IMAGES
of America

BOONE
COUNTY

This picture could have been taken on any number of Boone County farms in the first half of the twentieth century. A farmer attired in overalls stands with his mules, preparing for spring ploughing. One of the farm cats rubs against his leg, well fed from the morning's milking, while a chicken scratches in the dirt of the barn yard. Sterling Rouse, the farmer in this picture, owned a farm on Limaburg Creek Road, which is now part of the airport property. Each spring, Sterling could be found in his maple sugar camp, tapping maple trees and rendering the sap into maple syrup. Sterling was also well known for his horticultural skills; he often hosted representatives from the University of Kentucky Agricultural Department in his orchards. Sterling and his wife, Beulah, were well known and respected members of the Limaburg community.

IMAGES
of America

BOONE
COUNTY

Susan M. Cabot and Michael D. Rouse

ARCADIA
PUBLISHING

Published by Arcadia Publishing
Charleston, South Carolina

Library of Congress Catalog Card Number: 98-86343

For all general information contact Arcadia Publishing at:
Telephone 843-853-2070
Fax 843-853-0044
E-mail sales@arcadiapublishing.com
For customer service and orders:
Toll-Free 1-888-313-2665

Visit us on the Internet at www.arcadiapublishing.com

In 1817, George Anderson bought out a ferry operation located along the Ohio River in the most northern part of Boone County, along what is now called Route 8 or "River Road." The ferry provided an important and convenient link between Kentucky and Ohio. The Boone County river community of Constance developed in close proximity to the ferry. In 1865, after a series of owners, George Kottmyer purchased the successful operation. It remained in the Kottmyer family for over 120 years. Initially powered by two horses continuously walking a treadmill, the ferry boats progressed to feature steam engines in 1867 and, later, diesel engines. The Anderson Ferry has been in daily operation, except during flood times, since 1817 and today is one of only three full-time, year-round ferries running on the Ohio River.

Contents

ACKNOWLEDGMENTS

The authors would like to thank the following people, whose generous help in sharing their treasured photographs and knowledge of Boone County history made this book possible. Their willingness to offer insight into the county's past has made our job an enjoyable one. To all our contributors, a most sincere thanks! A special thank you is given to Elizabeth McMullen Kirtley, without whose assistance this book would not have been possible.

Thelma Anderson
Louise Aylor
Surface "Tuffy" Barlow
Boone County Historic Preservation
Helen Stephenson Brown
Bullittsburg Baptist Church
Luella and Allan "Bud" Burcham
Bernice Shinkle Craddock
Yvonne Hempfling Edwards
Dennis and Joella Sleet Flynn
Cindy Tupman Frederick
The William "Red" Garnet Family
William and Virginia Graves
Buddy Grubbs
JoAnn Nusbaum Hitzfield
Mrs. Charles Hollis
Pete and Alice Jarrell
Elizabeth McMullen Kirtley
Mark Kloeker
Virginia Nestor Kohl

Frances Siekman Kottmyer
Richard L. Kottmyer
Mary Jane Nusbaum
Linda Rouse Osborne
Mrs. Robert K. Porter
Corky and Imogene Regenbogen
Betty Weaver Roter
Ervan Rich
Jerry and Carole Richards
Katherine Tanner Rouse
Mr. and Mrs. Henry "Junior" Shinkle
Aline Shields Stephens
Ann Stephens
Evelyn Tanner
Glen Talbert
Anita Florence Cook Vice
The Albert Weaver Collection
    of Burlington Baptist Church
Charlotte Bradford Wilson
Kathleen Woods

INTRODUCTION

Boone County was established by the legislature of the Commonwealth of Kentucky in December 1798, with local government activity to commence on June 1, 1799. Located in the most northern portion of the state, the land that was to become Boone County had seen white settlement as early as 1789. People were drawn to Boone County because of its excellent access to the Ohio River and an abundance of fertile farmland. Kentucky also made a good stopping place for those pioneers traveling from Pennsylvania, Virginia, or North Carolina. In the late eighteenth century, the urge to move west was a popular challenge, but the conditions beyond Kentucky were still a little too unknown.

Boone County was built on faith, a belief in family, and respect for the land. Agriculture became the primary source of income, and the small industries that developed were almost entirely dependent on farm products. These business ventures included the development of several distilleries, many gristmills, sawmills, blacksmith shops, and later, creameries and rolling mills. In the early days, transportation centered around the Ohio River, and communities formed along the waterway at key ferry and shipping points. General stores became popular, often carrying any type of supplies the farmer could not grow or produce on the farm.

The first permanent public building in a settlement area was often a church. The founders of some of the earliest churches, such as Bullittsburg Baptist Church and Hopeful Lutheran Church, traveled from somewhere else as a body of believers to establish a church and a new home in a new place. The faith of these early settlers gave them the strength to persevere in difficult circumstances.

In 1998, Boone County's bicentennial year, this is the second fastest growing county in the Commonwealth of Kentucky. We have a major international airport that is helping to generate extensive industrial, commercial, and residential growth. This seemed like a good time to pause and reflect on Boone County's heritage, and photographs provide an enjoyable means to accomplish this goal.

Compiling a pictorial history of Boone County was both an easy and difficult task. Two hundred years of happenings, locations, and personages combine to form a rich and varied history. Beginning with prehistoric life at Big Bone Lick, many events have shaped the development of the county. The citizens of Boone County today have been very generous in sharing their stories and pictures. The opportunities for collecting pictures and local histories were so great that the choice became a difficult task. The pictures in this book are but a fraction of the many family portraits, candid snapshots, and landscape scenes that are waiting to be shared.

The photographs represent the time period from 1885 to 1945 in Boone County. They were chosen based on the theme of "Faith, Family, and Farming." The chapter titles reflect a relatively simple approach to life in Boone County during this time period. Our purpose in developing this book was threefold. First, we wanted to show our respect and appreciation to the early Boone Countians. Their commitment and hard work is a large part of the reason Boone County is prospering today. This book is for longtime residents of the county who fondly remember the Boone County landscape and life of their childhood. Finally, and perhaps most important of all, this book is for new Boone Countians who have no idea that Boone County was a very different place just 50 years ago. For everyone, we hope it offers insight into the county's history and heritage.

As the Boone County landscape is altered, old homesteads disappear and communities that once thrived change or become non-existent. Small-town postmarks such as Limaburg, Landing, and Crescent are a thing of the past. Farming, once a county-wide occupation, is now the exception. For those who have never farmed and those who grew up on a farm, these pictures offer a view into a lifestyle largely vanished from the county.

While land use is dramatically different, the faith practiced by those early settlers continues today. Many of the first churches established in Boone County continue to have strong, vibrant, and diversified congregations. Faith and fellowship remain significantly important parts of life in Boone County.

Education in Boone County has always been important, and the school system has evolved from one-room community schoolhouses. In the early days, graduation from high school was a major event for the whole family, and the proudly posed graduation pictures are the culmination of school days spent with cousins, neighbors, and friends in the community.

The support and joy of families remain a constant. Those large extended families provided a source of support and strength that, coupled with their faith, helped Boone Countians survive and prosper. Family pictures trigger pleasant memories and provide a good look at changing lifestyles.

Loyalty to a particular community was, and is, important to the citizens of Boone County. During this time period, it was essential that neighbors help each other and work together for the good of everyone. But beyond that, they truly enjoyed each other's company, and the childhood playmate of a neighboring family might well become a sweetheart and then a spouse. Practical entertainment such as quilting or community baseball rivalries each had their place in rural Boone County. Early Boone County businesses often supplemented the farm families. Local business owners often took farm produce in lieu of cash when the economy was tight. It was part of being one community.

A number of written sources have helped to preserve Boone County history. Two of the most useful sources in developing this book were the extensive writings of the late Boone County historian, William Conrad, and various editions of the *Boone County Recorder* from 1875 to 1945. Mr. Conrad's commitment to an accurate documentation of history makes publications like this possible.

We offer this book as a gift. Happy 200th Birthday, Boone County!

One

FAITH AND FELLOWSHIP

In 1793, twelve families from central Kentucky joined pioneers who had already made a home in the North Bend Bottoms along the Ohio River in what would become Boone County. In June 1794, they organized the Bullittsburg Baptist Church with the assistance of ministers John Taylor and Joseph Redding, and Elder William Cave from the Great Crossings Baptist Church in Scott County. Bullittsburg Baptist Church became the "mother" of all Boone County Baptist churches, and her members were among the most active community leaders. The first church building, built in 1797, was a log construction built on land donated by George Gaines. Several new Baptist congregations were formed in different parts of the county during the early years at Bullittsburg, including Woolper's Bottom (1801), Middle Creek (1803), and Sand Run (1819). In 1819, Woolper's Bottom Baptist rejoined Bullittsburg and a fine new brick sanctuary was constructed. The church, shown in this *c.* 1919 photograph, continues to serve the Bullittsburg Baptist Church congregation.

East Bend Baptist Church was constituted in 1819 after several members of Middle Creek Baptist Church requested permission and support to establish a new church in East Bend Bottoms. The church building, still in use today, dates to c. 1826. Much of the written church history was lost when the records were destroyed in a 1953 house fire.

Community fellowship is depicted in this 1917 picture of a church picnic at East Bend Methodist Church near Rabbit Hash. The boy in short pants and a cap (left foreground) is former county surveyor, Noel Walton. East Bend Methodist Church was founded c. 1860 and was one of several churches serving the faithful residents of the Ohio River community.

In April 1855, seven members of the Dry Creek Baptist Church were given letters of dismissal in order to establish a Baptist church in Florence. The church was built on a lot purchased from the Wilhoit family, who lived on Lexington Pike. Among the founding families were the Scotts, Snyders, Dulaneys, Stephens, and Finches. This building was used by the congregation until 1930, when the second church building was dedicated.

With the completion of the second Florence Baptist Church sanctuary, there were two Baptist church buildings on Main Street (Covington-Lexington Pike). This picture shows the location of the old church in relation to the 1930 building. In 1955, Sunday school rooms were built on the site of the first church. The 1930s building is still a part of the church complex.

The first Florence Methodist Church was located on Banklick Street. It was built by members of the congregation on a lot purchased for $80 from Samuel Craig in 1842. The building was renovated several times and served the congregation for over 80 years until the 1930s, when it was considered unsafe and was abandoned. In 1931, the church purchased a lot for a new building on Main Street.

Methodist Church   Petersburg, Ky.

The Petersburg Methodist Church was founded c. 1850, and a sanctuary was built on First Street. In the early, prosperous years of Petersburg, the Christian and Methodist churches had active congregations. Over time, the Methodist church lost membership, had a preacher only once a month, and finally closed in the mid-twentieth century. The brick church was demolished, but the cast-iron fence and many of the pews remain in Petersburg.

St. Paul's Roman Catholic Church had its beginning with the arrival of the Cornelius Ahrens family in Florence. Mr. Ahrens, a native of Ireland, found only three other Catholics in Florence when he arrived. St. Paul's was established shortly after Mr. Ahrens invited Rev. Thomas Butler of Covington to his home to say Mass and Mr. Ahrens suggested establishing a church. In 1855, Mr. Ezra Fish donated the land for the church on the corner of Shelby and Center Streets. On this lot, the men of the parish built a frame church that was dedicated in July 1856. The building measured 25 feet by 40 feet and had a 30-foot-tall steeple. A school was later established in the parish. This building was home to St. Paul's until the new church was built on Dixie Highway. The building on Shelby Street was often used for community gatherings such as Florence High School graduations.

The Walton Christian Church, established in 1873, met for a number of years in the lodge hall at Walton, or at the Stephenson Mill School. In 1879, they built a church on High Street using salvaged materials. The congregation moved in 1918 to this new brick church on Main Street. After a disastrous fire in 1947, Walton Christian Church was rebuilt on the 1917 stone foundation.

The Walton Methodist Church had its origins in 1879, during the ministry of Rev. W.W. Spats. The first church was dedicated in 1886 as Wall's Chapel on a lot just north of the old school. It served the congregation for 44 years, until the present church was built on South Main Street. The church was renamed Walton United Methodist Church in the 1930s.

14

In May 1843, Big Bone Baptist Church was formed with 42 members. From its inception to 1874, Brother Robert Kirtley served as pastor. Thomas Huey and John C. Riley were the first two deacons. Robert's son, James, assisted him in preaching and served as pastor from 1874 to 1900. The church building pictured here was built in 1857.

Pictured is the interior of Big Bone Baptist Church during World War II. It is a very accurate representation of worshippers in Boone County at the time. The ladies are attired in hats, and the men are dressed in suits and ties. The windows and doors are open to let in the breeze, and one can almost hear the slow back and forth swish of fans during the sermon.

After meeting for nearly one year in the local Grange Hall, the congregation was pleased to welcome the hundreds of people attending the dedication of the Bullittsville Christian Church in August 1880. The large new church cost $3,000, and the $600 outstanding debt was collected on that dedication Sunday, after a powerful sermon by Elder W.S. Keene. The service was followed by a traditional church picnic, which was held in a nearby locust grove.

Dinner Tab...

The Point Pleasant Christian Church dedicated its new church building on September 28, 1913. It replaced the old church building that was erected in 1841. The new church was organized through the efforts of Walter Scott with 61 founding members, including the Ellis, Walton, McGlasson, Cullom, Foster, and Riggs families. As in other rural communities, the church offered not only a source of religious strength but also a meeting place to socialize with other members of the community. As seen here, the ladies of the church made sure that members were well fed, both spiritually and physically, on the dedication day.

17

Union Baptist Church began as a branch of Big Bone Baptist Church. The Big Bone Church acquired land in Union in 1876 and erected a church building. In 1886, Union Baptist Church was organized with 35 members, and the property was transferred to the new church. The first pastor was Rev. Lafayette Johnson.

Union Presbyterian Church began in 1879 as an outreach ministry of the well-established Richwood Presbyterian Church. In 1885, a permanent Presbyterian congregation was established at Union, under the leadership of Rev. J. Walton Graybill. Founding members converted an old storehouse into a proper church building. Union Presbyterian Church is presently located just south of town.

18

Big Bone Methodist Church had its beginnings in 1887 when Rev. George Froh began preaching in an old barroom near the famous salt springs. A permanent church building was constructed in 1888 and served the Methodist congregation until the mid-1990s. The original church building, now owned by a Baptist congregation, is beautifully preserved with few changes since its late nineteenth-century construction.

In 1930, the Big Bone Methodist Church Ladies Aid Society had been active for over 35 years. Pictured here, from left to right, are as follows: (first row) Gerte Jones, Bertha Miller, Sallie Moore, Mrs. Kite, Winnie Aylor, Addie Burris, and Mrs. Elva Hughes; (second row) May Feldhaus, Mrs. Zimmerman, Sophia Jones, unidentified, Mrs. Alta Hamilton, Mrs. Hughes, Maggie Black, and Mary Judge.

Hughes Chapel Methodist Church, formerly located in Beaver, was established in 1878 by Rev. George Buffington. The first church building was an old grange hall purchased by J.C. Hughes Sr. In 1883, this new church was constructed and named in memory of Mr. Hughes. The church building was demolished *c.* 1976, but the Hughes Chapel Cemetery remains a well-preserved community landmark.

In 1883, a meeting was held by members of Baptist churches in the vicinity of Beaver Lick to consider organizing a Baptist church there. Beaver Lick Baptist Church was organized on November 3, 1883. The next year, Brother L. Johnson became pastor, and W.M. Rouse was elected clerk. In 1883, the church had 130 members. This building served the congregation until a new building was built on U.S. 42 in 1979.

The Gunpowder Baptist Church, also known as the Forks of Gunpowder Church, has a long and interesting history in Boone County. The church was first established in 1812 when 28 members of Bullittsburg Baptist Church from the Gunpowder Creek area asked to be dismissed for the purpose of establishing a church closer to home. Permission was granted, and Christopher Wilson became the first pastor of the Gunpowder Baptist Church. Although little is known for certain, the first building was apparently constructed of stone on an island in Gunpowder Creek. In 1840, the congregation declared themselves Predestinarian Baptists and became members of the Salem Association. The church building pictured here was built beside Gunpowder Creek in the early 1850s. In 1897, Gunpowder Baptist Church became defunct. The Burlington Baptist Church held a mission at the old Gunpowder Church in 1902, and it was determined that a church would be constituted. The church closed in 1939, due to a lack of members. The building still stands today, in use as a barn, on Pleasant Valley Road.

The Florence Christian Church, the earliest church in Florence, was organized in the 1830s. In 1842, a brick church building was completed on land owned by James Stephens. This "little white church" stood at the corner of Main Street and Dixie Highway for over 120 years. After the skirmish at Florence during the Civil War, the wounded were laid in the grass around the church.

When they entered Florence from the east, the first church travelers saw was the Presbyterian church. Located on the eastern end of a tree-lined Main Street beside the old town hall, it was part of the city's religious community for over 40 years. Due to declining membership, the church closed at the end of WW I and was sold in 1920.

The New Bethel Baptist Church of Verona was founded in 1840 at the home of Zadok Stephenson, who later donated land for a church building. Pictured is the second New Bethel Baptist Church, built and furnished in 1880 at a cost of $2,036. This building was located at the site of what is presently New Bethel Cemetery, just south of Verona.

St. Patrick's Roman Catholic Church in Verona began as a result of an influx of Irish immigrants to the southern part of the county. In 1865, John Dempsey donated a lot for the church, and St. Patrick's became a parish center. Eventually, All Saints Church in Walton, once a mission of St. Patrick's, became the primary Catholic church and St. Patrick's closed.

The 1830s were a time of change for Hopeful Lutheran Church. In 1835, the church's annual meeting minutes were recorded for the first time in English instead of German. Two years later, the congregation built a new brick church, after having worshipped for 30 years in log churches. This building was used by the congregation for 70 years until it was replaced by the present structure in 1917.

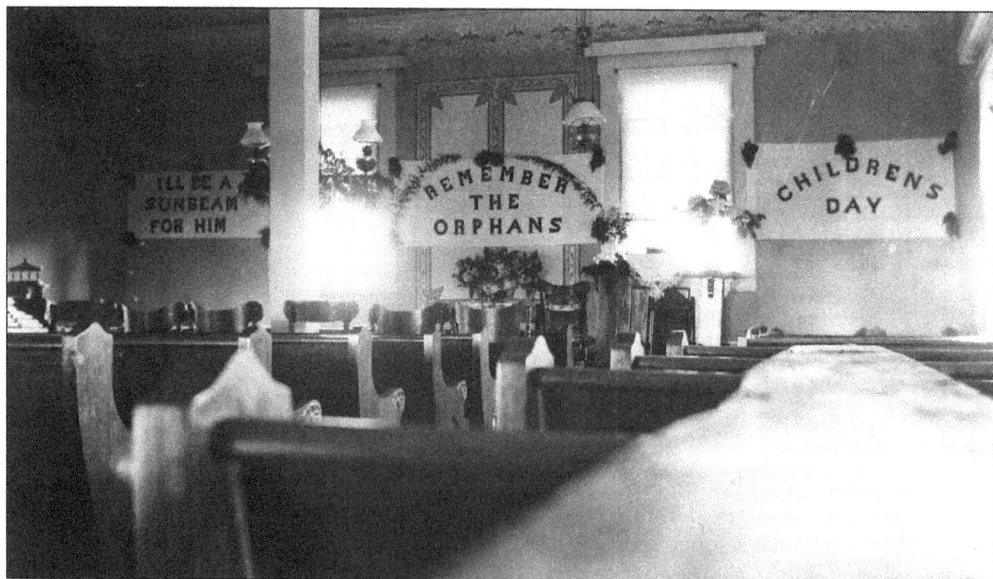

The Lutheran churches of Boone County traditionally celebrated "Children's Day" on the second Sunday in June. This picture shows the interior of Ebenezer Lutheran Church decorated for the celebration Sunday honoring the church's young members. Ebenezer Church, located on Mt. Zion Road, was founded in 1856. It was part of the Boone County Lutheran Charge until it merged with the Hopeful Church in 1932.

On January 21, 1854, Hebron Evangelical Lutheran Church was organized at the home of John J. Crigler by 16 members of Hopeful Lutheran Church who wanted a church closer to their homes, in the northern part of the county. The church was named for the mother church, Hebron Lutheran, in Madison County, Virginia. The Reverend David Harbaugh, pastor of the charge, made a trip back to Virginia to ask the congregation there for financial help in building the new church. His sermon on benevolence was successful, and he returned with $530. The church was built in less than one year and was dedicated in December 1854. From its founding until 1945, Hebron and Hopeful were a joint parish that shared one pastor. Pictured here is one of the lanterns mounted on posts leading from the church along Limaburg Road into the town of Hebron. After having served the community for over 100 years, this building was replaced by the present structure on the same site.

The Ladies Aid Society of Hebron Lutheran Church is pictured during a meeting in the early 1940s. Members, from left to right, are as follows: Dell Graves, Eva Goodridge, Stella Rouse, Lillie Conner, Grace Graves, Mannie Lodge, Alice McGlasson, Ella Getker, Mother Meyers, and Lucy Hauter. Lucy Hauter was the wife of the Reverend H.M. Hauter, pastor of the church.

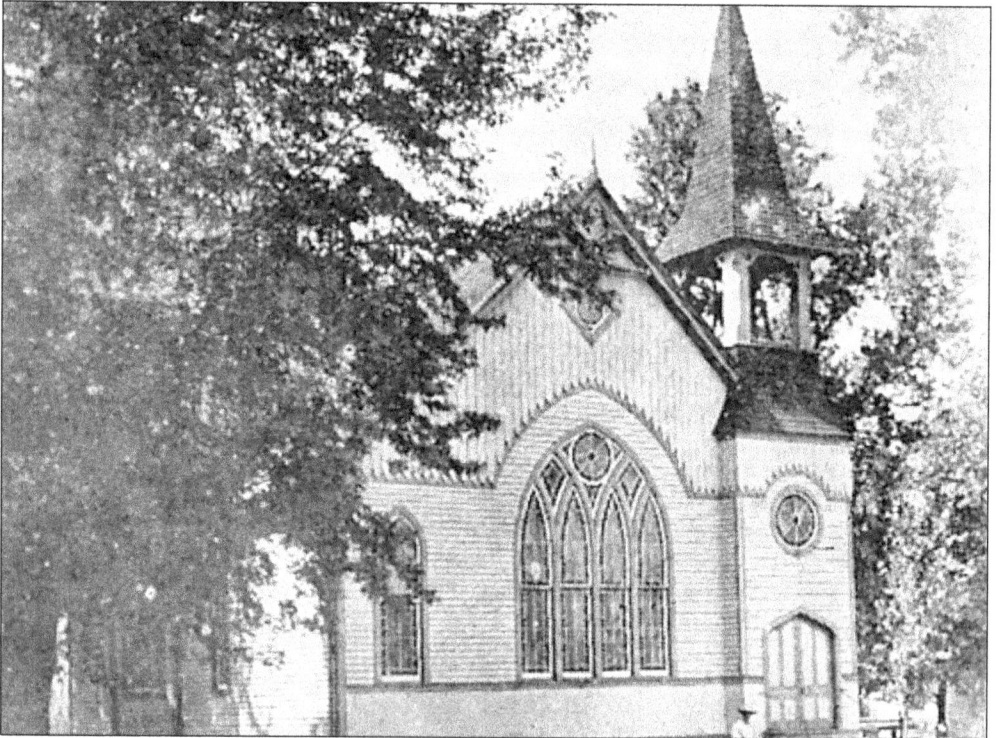

In 1842, with the blessings of Bullittsburg and Middle Creek Baptist Churches, the Burlington Baptist Church began meeting in the home of Squire Scott. Under the leadership of Pastor Robert Kirtley, the newly formed congregation, which included several African-American members, built a new brick church in 1843. The church building pictured was dedicated in December 1892 and remained in use until 1979.

The First Universalist Church of Burlington was organized in May 1876. The congregation met for several years at the Burlington Methodist Church before building a new sanctuary on Garrard Street. The church minutes documenting the November 1879 dedication service stated that this church building was "erected by loving hands and faithful hearts for the worship of God."

The Belleview Christian Church, founded in 1883, dedicated their new church building in 1884. The following week, the *Boone County Recorder* noted that the congregation that day may have been the largest crowd ever seen in Belleview. It was also reported that the new church building seemed rather small at times, but it continues to serve Belleview in the 1990s.

For over 75 years, the Lutheran churches of Boone County were members of a joint parish that shared one pastor. Members of Hopeful, Hebron, and Ebenezer were elected to a Joint Council that dealt with matters concerning the three congregations. Pictured here are members of the council, gathered in front of Ebenezer Lutheran Church on Mt. Zion Road. The church was located near what is presently the south-bound exit ramp of I-75.

By the 1930s, the congregation of Hebron Lutheran Church had added an education wing to the original wing of the 1854 church sanctuary. Hebron remained part of the joint parish with Hopeful Lutheran Church until 1945 when, during the pastorate of Rev. J. Paul Rimmer, both churches voted to dissolve the union and become independent charges.

In 1913, Point Pleasant Christian Church dedicated its new brick sanctuary. The church was organized in 1839 through the efforts of Walter Scott. Sixty-one members were present at the organizational meeting. The group met in the Point Pleasant Schoolhouse and in members' homes until the first church was built in 1841. The Christian Church in Constance was an offspring of Point Pleasant Church.

The original sanctuary of Bullittsville Christian Church was struck by lightning in 1910 and was nearly destroyed by the resulting fire. The members rebuilt the church pictured here on the same site. Bullittsville is another Boone County community that was once thriving with activity. Institutions such as the Christian Church carry on the community name.

On Sunday, November 11, 1917, the members of Hopeful Evangelical Church celebrated the dedication of their new sanctuary. Built during the pastorate of Rev. George Royer, it was the congregation's fourth church building to occupy the one-acre site on Hopeful Road. The contractor for the construction was George P. Nicholson of Walton. The contract price, not including art-glass windows, light, heat, frescos, and other furnishings, was $8,500. Ground was broken for the new building on June 13, 1917. The cover of the day's program reads that it was dedicated in honor of the quadri-centennial of the Protestant Reformation. For the occasion, Pastor Royer composed an original hymn entitled *Tressler*. Luncheon was served after the morning worship service and was followed in the afternoon by the Quadri-Centennial Rally. The day concluded with an evening worship service. To continue the celebration, services were held each evening of the following week. Harold Beemon, one of the young men present at the dedication, later entered seminary and became a Lutheran pastor. This building still stands on Hopeful Road.

Two

EDUCATION

The "Old" Burlington High School graduated its first class in 1911. Built as an early consolidated school, it served both students from Burlington and those from surrounding county areas. After finishing elementary school, some students boarded while attending Burlington since the distance from their homes made a daily trip impossible. The building stood near what is presently a ball field behind Burlington Elementary School. The school's PTA was very active, and in the 1920s, introduced innovations that are often taken for granted today. In 1927, the school began serving lunches and in 1929, installed water fountains. The last graduating class from this school building was the class of 1939. The nickname of the high school team was "the Burlington Tomcats."

The District 9 School was also known as the Pleasant Ridge School. Located at the northwest corner of Hopeful Road and U.S. 42, it operated for over 40 years until it consolidated with the Florence School in 1910. In 1875, the teacher at Pleasant Ridge School was paid $172.90 for a five-month school term of instruction for 41 students.

This picture may be from the early days of the Union School, located on the Union-Visalia Road, or what is presently Mt. Zion Road. The school was founded in 1869. Students walked or rode horses from the surrounding community and nearby farms. One of the little boys on the front row appears to have dressed up for his school picture—his friend seems ready for a good game of baseball.

In rural nineteenth-century Boone County, buildings often served several different purposes. In this case, the grange hall (part of a community called Grange Hall, and later, Buffalo) also served as the local school. Grange Hall is one of many small communities now vanished from the Boone County landscape. It was located near the intersection of Camp Ernst and Hathaway Roads. Pictured in this 1896 schoolhouse scene are, from left to right, as follows: (first row) Annie Portwood, Rachel Wilson, Cecile Gulley, Anna Carlisle, Ann McMullen, Grace Garrison, Allie Weaver, Grace Neal, Dell Utz, Imogene Neal, Lottie Garrison, Jessie Utz, Susie Adams, Bee Utz, Una Utz, Hattie Rouse, Will Rouse, Richard Rouse, Robert Rouse, and Will Kite; (second row) Laura Wolff (teacher), Joe Wilson, Lester Gulley, Tom Huey, Jim Huey, unidentified, Wilton Adams, Robert Williams, Harry Wilson, Owen McMullen, Claud Utz, Bill Williams, Douglas Rouse, Lewis Weaver, and Robert Carlisle.

Not all schools in Boone County were public schools. For a time, private schools flourished in the Florence area. One such school was in a large antebellum house located on Burlington Pike, at the end of Girard Street. A tuition receipt shows that William Henry Tanner paid $4.12 for 3/4 of a month of schooling for his three daughters in 1882. The building was demolished when Girard Street was extended to the new Burlington Pike.

This picture bears the inscription "Burlington 1912." It is likely that there were only four members of the Burlington School graduating class that year. In early twentieth-century Boone County, graduating from high school was a considerable accomplishment, primarily because of the time commitment it represented. A formal graduation portrait shows off new clothes and hothouse flowers.

These students are from the Locust Grove School on Locust Grove Road, just off East Bend Road, near Burlington. Perhaps the photographer came in this car, and the students and their teacher thought it would make a unique Boone County school picture. Remnants of the Locust Grove School remain today, in use as a storage building.

Between Verona and Walton, not far from Beaver, was the Stephenson Mill School. This rural schoolhouse, complete with a bell to call students, presents a picturesque view of early education in Boone County. The school may have been located on land owned or donated by the Stephenson family, who ran a large gristmill.

During the school year, Louise Jack traveled weekly from her Beaver home to attend school in Walton. She left her horse and carriage at the livery on North Main Street and spent the week with the Bedinger family or other Walton friends before going home to Beaver on the weekends. This picture is her 1921 graduation portrait.

Taking time out from readin,' writin,' and 'rithmetic, these 17 Pleasant Valley students and their teacher pose for this October 3, 1907 photograph. It must have been the middle of Indian summer, as their shirt sleeves and bare feet attest. As the county schools consolidated, Pleasant Valley students went to either Florence or New Haven.

Limaburg was located approximately halfway between Florence and Burlington, where Limaburg Road intersects Burlington Pike. In its heyday, the community of Limaburg included a general store, blacksmith shop, sawmill, gristmill, and school. Not only did the school give the children an education, it offered many social events such as ice cream socials and community spelling bees.

An early Hebron School was located on the east side of Limaburg Road, just before entering the town of Hebron. It was a well-built frame structure, somewhat more substantial than the schoolhouses in more rural areas of the county. The building survives today in two pieces, both of which have been remodeled into residences.

Students of the Pleasant Valley School (c. 1900) are, from left to right, as follows: (first row) Edna Houston, Edo Rouse, Flora Rouse, Sidney Rouse, Mart Beemon, Edna Barlow, Eugene Long, Ransom Vaughn, Louis Clegg, Lonnie Tanner, Kitty McHenry, Harvey Rouse, Richard Rouse, Nettie Sarah, Nettie Rouse, and Arch Rouse; (second row) Jim Beemon, Lizzie Rouse, Bessie Rouse, Jim Long, Eli Borders, Ethyl Tanner, Artie Borders, Harry Rouse, and Leslie Barlow; (third row) Sam Orem (teacher), Roland Rouse, Una Borders, Herb Rouse, Ed Borders, Jeannie Chrisler, Mae Chrisler, Lulu Rouse, Ervin Tanner, Newt Long, Linnie Easton, and Clint Beemon.

These Taylorsport students are gathered in front of their school in this early 1900s photograph. The village of Taylorsport was named for James Taylor, of the Campbell County Taylors, who started a ferry in 1836 on the upper side of Elijah's Creek. One of the teachers at Taylorsport school was Anita Hempfling, who taught at both the Taylorsport and Florence Schools.

Photographed in 1934, Burlington School's fifth and sixth grade students are, from left to right, as follows: (first row) Leroy Bethel, Bud McMullen, Marion King, unidentified, Jimmy Edwards, and Robert Ryle; (second row) Billy Walker, Robert Goodridge, Mary Snow, Lorraine Meyers, Rose Stephens, Elaine Vice, Ruth Woolet, Muriel Nichols, and Joseph Ring; (third row) Jesse Murray, Grace Freeman, Carolyn Cropper, Mildred Siekman, Ida Pearl Gulley, Florence Cook, Virgil Gulley, James Gale Smith, Leon Day, Daniel Ryle, Janet Brothers, Robert Gulley, and Edith Harris; (fourth row) Eli Hawn, Faustina Lea, Fannie Utz, Josephine Lea, Helen Demmler, Frances Finn, Tommy Sullivan, Russell Utz, and Mrs. Lamb (teacher).

Under the guidance of teachers Ralph and Molly Lents, the Constance School became the first Boone County elementary school to offer an eight-month session. Pictured in this early 1930s photograph are, from left to right, as follows: (front row) Martha Jackson, Emogene Austin, unidentified, Virginia Regenbogen, Alice Tunning, Wyonna Reeves, Thelma Heist, Mary Hood, and Mollie Lents (teacher); (second row) O.D. Heist, unidentified, Bill Megley, Raymond Jackson, Bill Peeno, Ralph Prabel, Vern Reeves, and Corky Regenbogen; (third row) Shelby North, George Tungate, Kenneth Rodamer, Wilbur Hood, Alvin McGlasson, Jim Crowley, and George Jackson.

The Belleview School was built in 1909 as one of Boone County's early consolidated schools. There was a movement to modernize the county's education system by making large schools, initially offering grades 1–12 in central locations. This c. 1925 class picture features Allan "Bud" Burcham (second from the right, top row). The Belleview School closed when Kelly Elementary School was opened.

These Point Pleasant School students are gathered on the front porch, waiting for school to begin. Photographed in early March, they are probably beginning to think of vacation; the school term then was shorter than today's nine-month term. Upon completing elementary school, Point Pleasant students went on to high school in either Florence or Hebron.

There was time for fun as well as learning in Boone County's country schools. Recess was a welcome relief for these boys, showing off for the camera at the Hathaway School (c. 1930). Pictured, from left to right, are as follows: Bob Smith, Otho Hubbard, Chester Butler, Bill Aylor, Shelton Love, unidentified, Lloyd Stephens, and Alfred Love.

This 1925 Verona High School class proudly poses for their graduation picture. The Verona High School was built in 1914, after a successful vote by the citizens, at a cost of just over $10,000. Students came from the community of Verona and daily from counties to the south by train.

The 1936 class of the Hebron School was the first to graduate under principal Chester Goodridge. Pictured here, from left to right, are as follows: (first row) Joe Peeno, Lalie M. Delph, Deliliah Dolwick, Frances Siekman, Vivian Hood, and Milton Rodamer; (second row) John Sebastian, Ruth Lancaster, Ruth Hodge Tanner, Anna Lucille Grant, Mary Catherine Bullock, Evelyn Conrad, and Dorothy Dunaway; (third row) Gertrude Randall, Wood Edwards, Earl Heinbach, Kenneth Wohrley, Edward Reinhardt, William Loze, Manlius Goodridge, Gene Jones, George Sprague, Orville Judy, Bessie Reeves, and Lucy Marie Souther.

With the American flag in the background, the Florence High School students stand with their teacher, Mr. Yealey, to be photographed in the early 1920s. This may have been the entire high school—the number of students in graduating classes at the time ranged from two to nine. As indicated by the flag, patriotism was a part of everyday school life.

What could be more fun than attending a school called Possum Path? This small but very proper group of students lived in the East Bend neighborhood of Boone County, and their teacher seems determined to have them behave appropriately. It is interesting to note the age range of the students pictured in this late-nineteenth-century photograph.

Faculty and students at Florence School are gathered behind their school building in this early 1920s photograph. Teachers were Mr. A.M. Yealey, Mrs. Huey, Miss Kelly, and Miss Castleman. The school graduated its first class in 1914 and served the community until 1932, when a larger brick school was built. In the background is the steeple of the first St. Paul's Roman Catholic Church, which stood at the corner of Center and Shelby Streets. The school was located behind what is presently Florence Elementary and was once used as the cafeteria for the new building. It was demolished at the beginning of WW II. Professor Yealey, who served as both the principal and a teacher for many years, was called out of retirement to teach during the war.

Three

FAMILY AND HOME

This c. 1910 picture of the Flynn family features parents, children, and animals in the yard of their home on Pennington Road, between Walton and Verona. Chairs from inside have been brought out into the fresh air, and Mrs. Emma Stephenson Flynn plays the guitar while baby Matthew watches the hunting dogs and his brothers. Marie has her doll to play with, and father Tom Flynn seems to be in deep thought. Oren and Leo hold onto what appears to be a calf and a miniature donkey. A lone sheep grazes contentedly nearby. In early twentieth-century rural Boone County, it isn't always easy to know who might be taking the picture. One of the neighbors or family members may have had a camera, or itinerant photographers may have visited local farms trying to drum up business.

Seen in this c. 1890 photograph is the Shinkle family from the Woolper Creek area of Boone County. A formal family portrait such as this was quite an undertaking for a conservative, country farm family. Residents of western Boone County probably crossed the Ohio River via ferry to a studio in Lawrenceburg or Aurora, Indiana, for this type of photograph.

This photograph of the T.B. Rouse homestead on Conrad Lane is from a picture album owned by Frank Rouse. As with many homes through the county, cedar trees were planted in the front yard. Cedars often lined the drive to the house or were seen grouped in the family cemetery near the house. Although no fence surrounds the yard, the elaborate gate once welcomed guests to the home. The house was demolished in 1991.

Joel Tanner built this two-story brick home in the early 1850s on his farm, located between present-day Hopeful and Mall Roads, near Florence. Joel married Lydia Crigler in 1829, and the couple had 13 children together. Joel died at the age of 94 in 1902, and the house was inherited by his daughter and son-in-law, Almedia and Ezra Tanner. The house became home to four generations of the Tanner family.

Five generations of the Aylor family gathered in their home at Gunpowder to have this picture taken. Pictured from left to right, the family members are as follows: (seated) L.P. Aylor (holding granddaughter, Martha), unidentified young boy, E.D. Aylor, unidentified young boy, and Fannie Tanner; (standing) Rosa Aylor, Lully Tanner, Shelly Aylor, and Benjamin C. Tanner.

In this picture, Samantha Griffith Jackson, granddaughter of Rev. William Carpenter, looks more like a girl from a western town than a young lady in Richwood. Many of the families who lived along the Lexington Pike provided her with playmates, and she eventually married Lorenzo Jackson.

Lorenzo Jackson; his wife, Samantha; and his brother-in-law, Charles Griffith, ran the general store in Richwood. Located across from the Richwood Depot, as the railway prospered, so did the store. The general store was much like its counterparts across Boone County. Richwood was an important depot for the railroad.

H. Max Lentz referred to this picture as "Old Kentucky Home" in his book, *A History of Lutheran Churches in Boone County*. Susan Crigler Rouse, holding the family Bible, sits before the fireplace in her home near Limaburg (at what is presently the site of Heritage Bank). Susan was the daughter of Rev. Jacob Crigler, the second pastor of Hopeful Lutheran.

Pictured here are Young Nora and Myrtle Beemon. In a time when the infant mortality rate was high, parents had their babies and young children photographed in order to have a remembrance of them. Often, in the case of death, a photographer would be called in to photograph the child in the coffin. These kinds of pictures, combined with a lock of hair, were considered fitting memorials to the deceased. Happily, both of these young girls lived to adulthood.

Edward Snyder and Rhoda Tanner Snyder are posed for a very formal portrait. As was often the case in such studio photographs, the man is seated and the woman stands behind him. Couples traveled to Covington or Cincinnati to have their portraits made. Their family home was on Main Street in Florence, where the Baptist church is now located.

Sunday was a day of rest in nineteenth-century Boone County. After attending church, Sunday afternoons were a time of visiting and socializing. In this photograph, the Tanner and Olsner families enjoy a game of croquet in the yard of the Olsner home. The house, located on Main Street in Florence, stood on what is presently part of the Christian Church complex.

This home on Banklick Street in Florence stood near what is presently the drive-through of Bank One. In the background is a barn, the site of which is now part of the Dixie Highway. The house was one of the last on Banklick before the street became farm fields. A swing and a grape arbor was often found in many side and backyards of homes of the time.

Every well-appointed Boone County home of the nineteenth century had a parlor. It was the room set aside for special occasions and decorated with the best the family had. In this c. 1890 photograph are Carrie and Cora Tanner, daughters of Henry and Lucy Tanner, in the family parlor of their home on Main Street in Florence.

51

Seen in this picture is the Thomas Jackson Walton family, sitting in front of their home on Belleview Road. They are, from left to right, as follows: Eliza Hunt Walton (holding her daughter, Helen) Ruth, Alice, Joe, and Bill Walton. The scrollwork on the porch is typical of homes of the period. Alice Walton married Dr. M.A. Yelton and assisted with his medical practice in Burlington.

Fannie Belle Allen Adams grew up close to the western Boone County community of Normansville. In 1874, she married Bluford Watson Adams, who joined the Confederate Army at age 16 against his parents wishes. After living in the Normansville area for years, Mr. and Mrs. Adams moved to Burlington, where Bluford served as Boone County circuit court clerk.

Mary Lindsey Hume was the daughter of Will and Nell Hume. The Hume family initially settled in the southern part of Boone County, lending their name to a community that developed along the Cincinnati-Louisville Road. Mary most likely decided that her favorite doll must also be in the picture. Nell Hume may have heated a curling iron over the fire to make Mary's lovely corkscrew curls.

When Albert Dringenburg's father retired from farming and moved to Cresent Springs, Albert met Gertrude Eubanks, whose family lived in town. In 1906, they were married and had their wedding picture made at the Studio Grand in Cincinnati. Mrs. Dringenburg's hat is typical of the elaborate creations of the time. The couple lived on a farm on Burlington Pike, near the present-day location of Greenview Baptist Church.

Although many of Boone County's earliest residents were German, a substantial Irish community developed in Verona in the mid-nineteenth century. This *c*. 1895 Queen Anne house was the early twentieth-century home of Patrick E. Farrell, one of Verona's leading citizens. Farrell, born and raised in Boone County, was on the board of directors at Verona Bank and an active member of St. Patrick's Catholic Church.

Grandmother Martha Cason Jones enjoys taking a break in the sunshine while visiting with her daughter, Bessie Jones Stephens, and her young son, Lloyd. Boone County families usually lived close enough together to enjoy visits like this. Young people met through church events, at neighborhood parties, or through other family members. When they married, they often lived nearby.

Manley and Robert Gulley of Petersburg are pictured here, proudly showing off their new car. The Gulley boys, like most of their neighbors, were probably more familiar with nearby Indiana communities than they were with the rest of Boone County. Petersburg is almost directly across the river from Lawrenceburg, Indiana. In the nineteenth and early-to-mid-twentieth centuries, residents of both towns shared community resources via a convenient ferry.

Elizabeth Dell and her uncle, George Goodridge, pose with the family dog in this c. 1914 photograph. The picture was taken in front of the William H. Goodridge home, located just north of Florence on Goodridge Drive. The Goodridge family were large local landowners, and figured prominently in the nineteenth-century history of Florence.

The wedding of Shelly Aylor and Gertrude Michels was certainly an elegant occasion. The groom wears fashionable gloves with his three-piece suit, and the bride's floor-length gown and veil are enhanced by her large bouquet of roses. Gertrude was the daughter of Martin and Barbara Michels and Shelly was the son of Lewis and Rosa Aylor.

Even in early twentieth-century Boone County, the ladies of the community maintained some independence. Annie Sullivan McMullen is pictured with a favorite horse. Her husband, Asa, was Boone County clerk for many years, and both were active in community affairs.

This well-kept farm was the home of Willie and Fannie Utz. It stood on the northeast corner of Burlington Pike and Greenview Road. This view, captured during the early years of this century, shows that rural mail delivery had already begun, and the family no longer needed to call the post office for their mail. The small house in the background was the summer kitchen.

When WW I ended on November 11, 1918, the citizens of Boone County celebrated the return of peace in a variety of ways. In many churches throughout the county, bells were rung for several hours to spread the news and commemorate the victory. Neighboring farmers Liston Hempfling and Lloyd McGlasson took time off from their ever-present farm work on November 12, 1918, to celebrate the armistice.

William C. Walton of Burlington was quite young when WW I came along, but he willingly served his country. Traveling to Europe and enduring the difficult circumstances of war must have been a sobering experience for a young man from rural Boone County. Walton was undoubtedly glad to return home alive and resume his old way of life with a more mature perspective.

Patriotism ran high during America's involvement in WW I. Sixteen young men from Boone County died serving their country. Sorrow and pride in their actions were felt by the citizens of the county, and their relief and happiness on hearing the news of peace on November 11, 1918, was genuine and widespread. Adults and children alike found their own ways to celebrate. In Florence, five young boys took turns ringing the bell of the Presbyterian church all day to spread the good news. On their farms along the Ohio River, the children of Liston Hemplfing and Lloyd McGlasson joined their fathers in the November 12 celebration. With a large American flag attached to the back of the wagon, Ben McGlasson pulls passengers Vaughn Hempfling (left) and Paul McGlasson (right). A second flag flies atop a fence post in the background.

This c. 1920 photograph may be the wedding portrait of William and Patty Vest Waller. Both came from well-known southern Boone County families. Their ancestors and descendants have played a significant role in the overall success of Boone County, especially in the Walton-Verona area.

Well into the twentieth century, horse and mule-drawn vehicles were widely used for transportation in Boone County. Most roads were unpaved and, in many instances, followed creek beds. Even those families who owned automobiles often had to have them pulled from mud by a team of horses or mules. Pictured are Liston Hempfling and his son, Vaughn, near Taylorsport.

This c. 1919 photo shows a typical young family in the Hathaway neighborhood of Boone County. Hiram Stephens poses with his wife, Bessie Jones Stephens, and their son, Lloyd, in front of a simple yet picturesque late-nineteenth-century home. The question is, did the chicken just wander into the picture, or did she consider herself part of the family?

This lovely 1929 family portrait features the Joseph Weaver family of Longbranch Road, in Union. Photographed in 1929, proud parents Joseph and Ella Adams Weaver pose with their daughters, Sarah and Betty Jo. Both girls became popular Boone County teachers. Betty Jo Weaver Roter, living today in Williamstown, has written memoirs that give fascinating insights into life in early twentieth-century Boone County.

Taken from the Albert Rouse family album, this picture bears the caption, "We love the water." Enjoying the water of Fowler Creek near Union are Dudley Rouse; his mother, Luella (left); and his aunts, Atilla and Mary B. (right). The picture was taken around 1925, when the family was living in the old tollhouse on the Union-Florence Pike.

Women on Boone County farms led demanding, work-filled lives. Taking care of large families (and livestock), washing, cooking, and canning took up much of their time, yet they seemed to find time to plant and maintain some type of flower garden. As daughters married and moved away, they took starts of plants for their own garden. Pictured amidst her flowers is Mary Noell.

On April 26, 1887, John T. Stephenson of Walton and Lenora E. Houston of Verona were married at New Bethel Baptist Church by Rev. Lafayette Johnson. They eventually had eight children. In this picture, they are seen in front of their home on Burlington Pike, near Limaburg. Mr. Stephenson was so respected and liked in the Limaburg community that he was always referred to as "Neighbor" Stephenson.

Whether gospel hymns were sung unaccompanied at a prayer meeting or popular songs played on a pump organ in the parlor, music was a cherished part of the county's life. Before the days of recordings, radios, and TV, live performances by musicians enriched many social occasions. Members of the Waters family shown here, from left to right, are as follows: Addie, Stella, Earl, Bill, Oliver, and Lou.

This handsome gentleman was obviously the much loved and respected patriarch of his family. Alfred Cason was from the East Bend neighborhood of Boone County. Families were large and depended on one another for moral support, friendly advice, and social interaction. Family gatherings were a popular pastime, either in celebration of a special event or simply getting together for Sunday dinner.

In the 1930s river community of Petersburg, a very young Pete Jarrell bounces on the knee of his uncle, John Snelling. Extended families, including grandparents, aunts, uncles, and several generations of cousins, have always been an important part of the social structure of Boone County. Snelling lived in a small stone house, which is thought to have been built by the town's founder, John Tanner, c. 1795.

Young animals and children seemed to be natural playmates and friends on Boone County farms. Here Howard, Reuben, and Marie Kirtley pose with some friendly lambs at the family farm in East Bend Bottoms. Since the earliest days of Boone County history, members of the Kirtley family have been active community participants and leaders.

Birthdays have always been an occasion to bring families together to celebrate. Here the Tanner family celebrates the combined birthday party of Clifford Tanner and his daughter, Katherine, on Labor Day weekend in 1941. Pictured from left to right are as follows: (turning) Frank Beemon; (front row) Ruth Beemon, Carolyn Aylor, Mary Lou Dringenburg, Clyde Aylor, and Harold T. Dringenburg; (back row) Louise Aylor, Katherine Tanner, Wendell Aylor, and Charles Aylor.

During WW II, young Pete Jarrell of Petersburg was given the important task of caring for his uncles' fox hunting dogs, Glory, Beauty, and Doughboy, while the men were away fighting for America. It is likely that this was a welcome family responsibility and a way for Pete to feel like he was also part of the war effort.

In the nineteenth century, steamboat travel was the main means of transport for passengers and cargo. As it was replaced by the faster moving train systems, the steamboat became a leisurely means of recreational travel. The *Island Queen* was a famous craft that transported visitors up and down river to the Coney Island Amusement Park. In this 1941 picture, Anita Hempfling watches the boat pass by the family farm near Taylorsport.

In the early 1940s, the four Vice sons, Cline, James, Virgil, and Keith pose with their father, Lee Roy, in front of the family home on a branch of Woolper Creek. Virgil raised his family in a log house, located just down the road from his parents. The land along the creek was fertile, but often rocky and difficult to farm.

This informal portrait was probably made in the front yard of this farm couple's home. A rug has been spread over the grass, and a coverlet is suspended behind them. They appear happy and content in their years of married life.

Four

COMMUNITY

In the early 1900s, the village of Gunpowder appeared quiet as the photographer stood on an overlooking hill to make this picture. Gunpowder was, at one time, a thriving and active community. In the center of the picture is the general store, and above the store on the hill is the home of L.P. Aylor. A sawmill is seen in the foreground, along Gunpowder Creek, and a gristmill and blacksmith shop complete the businesses of the community. Until 1907, there was a post office at Gunpowder. Although the community had no churches, Gunpowder Baptist and Hopeful Lutheran churches were in the general area. Previously the town had been called "Pinhook" and "Sugartit." By the time the century changed, the chosen name for the area was Gunpowder. Students in the neighborhood attended the Pleasant Ridge School (or Pleasant Valley School), farther up the hill, towards Florence.

The Old Town Hall in Florence served several purposes in its long history on Main Street. Author John Uri Lloyd writes of his parents teaching there when the building was used as a school. When used as a town hall it was a polling place, where before the arrival of the secret ballot in 1892, the clerk would read out the voter's name and he would respond with his choice of candidate.

This hand-written invitation appears to have been for an exclusive party at one of Burlington's small hotels in 1888. Newspaper ads from the time indicate that the Boone House was quite elegant. Although most of the community entertainment was centered around family, church, or the sport of baseball, small parties such as this were also popular in the larger towns.

Main St. and Blacksmith Shop — Constance, Ky.

In the 1880 census, Constance is listed as having a population of 133. The picture shows the many businesses that lined Route 8 as it ran through Constance. Blacksmiths, a wagon maker, butcher, painter, stone mason, and retail merchant are some of the craftspeople listed in the census. Herds of hogs and cattle were often driven through the town on their way to the ferry, to be taken to the stockyards in Cincinnati.

This is a view looking west on Hebron's Main Street. Originally called Briar Patch, Hebron is named for the local Lutheran church. This early twentieth-century postcard shows a wide, tree-lined street with the blacksmith and carriage shop and Bullock's General Store. The twenty-first century will bring the new challenge for Hebron, with a rapidly growing Cincinnati/Northern Kentucky International Airport.

When traveling on the Lexington Pike from Cincinnati to Lexington, one of the most fashionable places to lodge for the night was the Southern Hotel, on the corner of Main and Youell Streets. In the 1883 *Atlas of Boone County*, the business reference lists Mrs. E.V. Grant as proprietor. She purchased the site from Jonathan and Almira Williams in 1868.

This turn-of-the-century picture of First Street in Petersburg shows the almost boulevard size of the main streets in Petersburg. The postcard view, taken from the central business district on First Street, features the Methodist church on the left. It also gives an indication of the diversity of housing that could be found in Petersburg at the time.

Yourself and Company
are cordially invited to attend
A Select Leap Year Party, given by
the Young Ladies of Burlington
at Morgan Academy Hall,
May Thirteenth,
1892.

Music from the City.   *Supper at eleven o'clock.*

This is a very formal invitation for late-nineteenth-century Boone County. Morgan Academy was a private school in Burlington that once stood beside the Burlington Cemetery on what is presently Bullittsville Road. "Music from the City" may have referred to either Covington or Cincinnati, and it was certainly an enticement to attend the dance. It is certain that the young ladies and their guests were well chaperoned.

The Boone County Fair at Florence had its origins with the formation of the North Kentucky Agricultural Association in 1895. An amphitheater, with a bandstand in the center of the ring, was built on the corner of Lexington and Union Pikes, on land rented from William Perry Carpenter. In 1907, admission to the fair was 25¢. The main entrance was across from what is presently St. Paul's Church.

The original site occupied by the Florence Fair was a heavily wooded area called Carpenter's Woods. As the fair developed, many large trees were left to give shade to the fairgrounds. The first fair was held on September 3, 4, and 5, 1896, and for the next 36 years, it was a source of pride and enjoyment to the citizens of Boone County.

74

Part of the excitement of the Florence Fair was the yearly competition in categories such as floral arrangements, baking, and preserving. In this picture, the quilts in the background and the jars of canned goods are about to be judged. In 1914, the competition must have been strong—Judges Mrs. Rector, Mrs. Perry Allen, and Mrs. Cowen noted that they had a difficult time deciding between who should receive the blue and red ribbons.

Each year, the Boone County Fair at Florence offers a chance to see old friends and socialize. Seen here enjoying the fair is Rosa McMullen, standing in front of the merry-go-round. Before 1906, the ride was called the Flying Dutchman. Coca-Cola was sold for the first time at the fair in 1918. The cost of admission was 30¢, and the price of dinner was 40¢ per person.

There is no clear identification on this picture, but certain names and other clues on the back seem to indicate that this may have been a turn-of-the-century reunion of Union veterans of the Civil War in the tiny river community of Landing. Although Boone County primarily supported the Confederacy, some local men fought for the Union.

In 1906, Scott Chambers joined B.B. Allphin in the livery and undertaking business at Walton. Thus began the legacy of the Chambers family as Boone County funeral directors. Mr. Chambers's daughter, Mary Scott, became the first licensed female embalmer in the Commonwealth of Kentucky. An entry in the funeral home records dated 1925 reads, "This body was embalmed by Mary Scott, the first call she ever answered by herself and she done a fine job. Signed Papa."

VIEW.OF.PETERS.BURG.KY

This is an early-twentieth-century view of Tanner Street in Petersburg, looking west toward the Ohio River and Indiana. Petersburg, founded in 1789, was the first community in what was to become Boone County. Its prominent Ohio River location had also been the site of several prehistoric Indian villages. The river aided Petersburg in its nineteenth-century prosperity, especially after the Boone County Distilling Company was founded c. 1835. This postcard showcases several important buildings that have become Petersburg landmarks. The church steeple on the left belongs to the Petersburg Christian Church, built in 1840 and still in active use. The c. 1885 millinery shop was beside the church, and diagonally across from it, was a c. 1840 building that housed the town butcher on the first floor, then the Sons of Temperance, and later, the Masons (on the second floor). The wide, tree-lined streets with sidewalks are indications of a well-designed community.

One of Burlington's favorite sons, Albert "Sickem" Weaver poses on Washington Street in the county seat. As the center of government in Boone County, Burlington became the first local community to be incorporated in 1824. The charter was annulled in 1923, and today, Burlington is one of only two unincorporated county seats in the Commonwealth of Kentucky.

During the twentieth century, the Boone County section of the Ohio River has only frozen three or four times. Severe weather disrupted shipping and daily life because the river ferries could not run. It was, however, great fun for local citizens who dared to venture out on the frozen expanse. In the deep freeze of 1918, cars could cross the frozen river without a problem.

Thomas Zane Roberts, a local farmer, teacher, and inventor, was serious about the time he spent in church on Sundays. Around 1909, after he accidentally missed a Sunday, Roberts began to study the heavens from his Middle Creek home and made the calculations necessary to design and build this amazing solar clock. Robert's 8-foot-tall clock, which still works accurately, is housed at the Heritage Bank in Burlington.

Patriotism was alive and well in Boone County during WW I. In 1917, these Red Cross ladies were undoubtedly part of the auxiliary that was active in the Carlton Precinct. This ceremony at Rabbit Hash would have been a good time to raise funds for war relief efforts. The Boone County chapter of the Red Cross had 1,500 members and raised over $1,000 that year.

In August 1917, a severe thunderstorm and heavy winds destroyed the bridge at Limaburg. A vital link in the flow of traffic between Florence and Burlington, the bridge was soon rebuilt with the help of the men of the community. They are seen here, surveying the damage to the bridge's stone foundation. The Farrell home can be seen in the top left.

"O you bunch of old chickens," reads the inscription on the back of this photograph. The ladies are in-laws and neighbors of the Beemon and Tanner families. Women often came together for a day of quilting. One type of quilt was the friendship quilt. When one was completed, each lady embroidered her name on the quilt, forming a lasting record of the circle of friends and relatives.

Baseball was an American tradition that Boone County took seriously. Each community had a team, and the rivalries were intense. Some teams such as Hebron, pictured here in the 1920s, and Petersburg reached semi-professional status. Players were carefully chosen for their particular skills so that all positions would be covered. There were Saturday and Sunday afternoon leagues, as well as a church league that played on Saturday. Local baseball games were the talk of the community, and a pastime many citizens appreciated and looked forward to. The baseball teams had to raise money for equipment, umpires (who came from Cincinnati), and sometimes, for rent of a ballfield. They passed the hat at games or sponsored events such as picnics or fish fries to raise the necessary funds. William "Red" Garnett, pictured in the center of this postcard, was undoubtedly pleased to travel with the team and serve as the batboy.

Split Rock Kentucky on the Ohio River.

Split Rock, a tremendous glacial rock formation in the Ohio River near the mouth of Woolper Creek, was a popular gathering place for picnics and afternoon outings. Many groups arrived by boat and others walked or rode their bikes for a fun day among the prehistoric rocks.

Clint Jones of Union was one of many Boone County residents who made special trips for drinking water from the salt spring at Big Bone Lick. In prehistoric times, this famous salt spring drew mammoths and mastodons that subsequently perished in the boggy soil surrounding the spring. Much later, Big Bone became a popular gathering place for those who believed the waters had healing properties.

With the advent of the silent movie, citizens of the county were able to experience a new type of entertainment. At about the same time these films were introduced, the Presbyterian church in Florence closed and became a silent film theater known as the "show house." Note the addition of billboards on either side of the doors. When "talkies" came along, the theater closed and the building was remodeled.

The man in this photograph is identified as Reverend Twinkle, speaking at Rabbit Hash in 1917. The Rabbit Hash General Store, clearly visible in this picture, was built c. 1831 and is still in business in the same building. It remains a community gathering place, as is evident with this audience that includes men, women, children, and dogs.

These two ladies, Charlotte Bradford (of Gunpowder) and Mary Black (of Richwood), are at the height of 1920s fashion. Their bobbed hair and raised hemlines show that many young ladies of Boone County were becoming "modernized."

Yourself and Company

are cordially invited to attend a

Select Dance

at Ideal Theatre, Petersburg, Ky.,

Friday Evening, Jan. 30, 1920

Music:

Piano, Saxophone, Traps

Committee:

Early Mathews,
Stephens, Berkshire,

The Ideal Theater in Petersburg, also known as Gordon's Hall or the Petersburg Opera House, was the center of entertainment in this historic river community since its construction in 1896. The musicians for this particular event may have come from across the river in Lawrenceburg or Aurora, but the committee names listed are solid Boone County.

Richwood Station was a stop on the railway between Cincinnati and Lexington. The depot was located across from the intersection of Richwood Road and Lexington Pike (U.S. 25). The Richwood community also included a general store and the Richwood Deposit Bank, pictured here. The Lampton School lay south of Richwood.

Florence native Dr. Frank Sayre began his practice in Hebron in the early 1890s and continued to practice medicine for over 35 years. In the days when muddy roads made travel difficult, Dr. Sayre set out on his horse, Fannie, early in the morning to visit his patients and often worked well into the evening. In 1917, Dr. Sayre and his wife, Mabel, returned to Florence, where he continued to practice medicine.

Coming down Mile Hill from Hebron, a lovely panorama unfolds. Boone County's gently rolling hills and broad valleys are part of its age-old charm. In this view, the old Constance School and a community residence are visible through the trees. Admiring a picture of this scene is much safer than trying to catch the same view and navigate Mile Hill at the same time.

Friends and neighbors often gathered at a local business to pass on news or to pass the time. Friends pictured here, from left to right, are as follows: Jim Sleet, Allie Roter, Wendell Rouse, and Ward Sleet. The men are talking in front of the Beaver General Store, next to the garage. Each of these families have extensive histories in the Beaver and Walton sections of the county.

Ivan Rich and his mother, Vera, pose in the doorway of their Rabbit Hash home (*c.* 1926). Ivan's father, Jacob, operated the local blacksmith shop. Located on the left side of the road, about a quarter of a mile past the Rabbit Hash General Store, their home was destroyed in the flood of 1937.

In the early twentieth century, Walton's Main Street resembled much newer towns in the west, with its frame, false second-story storefronts and board sidewalks. The community was heavily damaged by fire some years later. The second floor of the 1906 Walton Hall (right foreground) has been the home of the Walton Masonic Lodge since the building's construction.

Perhaps no other Boone County community has seen as many changes in its streetscape as Union. This *c.* 1930 view, looking north down U.S. 42 from the corner of Mt. Zion, shows the old hotel and the old Presbyterian church on the west side. In the early twenty-first century, Union will change again as U.S. 42 is widened and rerouted around the original town center.

Arthur "Red" Jones built this car so that he and his brother Alfred "Pete" Jones could deliver the mail along a rural route. The car was apparently a big success—their friends and a neighborhood child and dog seem anxious to join in the picture. The Jones brothers are good examples of the fact that almost everyone in early twentieth-century Boone County had some sort of nickname.

In 1920 came the founding of the Hebron Deposit Bank. The first bank building was located on Route 20 ,and according to a 1930 article in *The Boone County Recorder*, "a safe was installed as near burglar-proof as possible to produce." Bank officers, from left to right, were as follows: (front row) Lenora Graves, Joel Clore (president), and Grace Rice; (back row) Benjamin B. Grant, Henry Getker, Frank Hossman Sr., Wilford M. Rice, William Goodridge Sr., Hubert Conner, John B. Cloud, Cleveland Hankin, Clinton S. Riddell, and Dr. Lewis C. Hafer. Of all the small community banks that did business in Boone County, Hebron is the last to remain independent, having never merged with other banks.

The PTA members gathered in front of the Constance School, are from left to right, as follows: (front row) Mrs. Zimmer, unidentified, Mrs. Pottenger, Mr. Lents, Mrs. Lents, Mrs. H. Kottmyer, and Mrs. George Kottmyer; (second row) Lottie Fisher, Mrs. Nell Kottmyer, Mrs. Charles Hodges, Mrs. Loze, Mrs. Klastner, Mrs. Peeno, and Sister Hamilton; (third row) Mrs. Reeves, Anna Dolwick, Tillie Hempfling, Mrs. Alferd Dolwick, unidentified, Mrs. Ray Cravens, and George Kottmyer; (fourth row) Erma Dolwick, Louise Klastner, Ruby H., Mrs. Riggs, Elizabeth Loze, unidentified, Son Kottmyer, and Brother Hamilton.

Nathaniel E. Riddell, the son of Fountain and Louisa Riddell, was born and raised in Burlington. After having studied law at what is presently the University of Cincinnati, Riddell returned to his hometown, where he became county attorney in 1906 and county judge in 1920. Under his leadership, toll gates were removed from county roads, a new jail was built, and the courthouse was furnished with a new heating system.

In 1937, an Ohio River flood devastated Northern Kentucky and the greater Cincinnati area. The river flooded many times before, but never quite this high or for this long. Homes, barns, outbuildings, and livestock were washed away, and entire communities all but disappeared. Here, the Kottmyer house at Anderson Ferry in Constance is more than halfway submerged.

Dr. M.A. Yelton and his wife, Alice, were a well-known couple in Boone County. During the hard times of the Depression, Dr. Yelton could be counted on to make house calls at any time of day or night to attend the sick, often taking farm produce as payment. In this photograph, the Yeltons are seen on Jefferson Street in Burlington. The old Presbyterian church is seen in the background.

In the first half of this century, many babies were still delivered at home. Physicians such as Dr. Nunnley brought many Boone County babies into the world. For having just delivered a baby, Dr. Nunnley appears very dapper in his bow tie, jacket, and white pants.

Five

FARMING

In this photograph, Wilton Stephens shyly (but proudly) shows off his young calf. A family friend, James Jones, can be seen in the background. Growing up in farming communities, Boone County children, especially boys, learned early about the responsibility of raising animals. During his 1918–1924 tenure, Boone County Agricultural Extension Agent Sutton began organizing young people into 4-H clubs. Under the guidance of the next extension agent, Holly Forkner, 10 community clubs were organized in Boone County. The term "4-H" stands for head, heart, hands, and health. In the early days, young women were taught primarily sewing and cooking, while young men concentrated on raising farm crops and animals. Teaching was, and still is, done by volunteers from the community. Examples of 4-H projects were exhibited at the county fair, where the animals raised would be shown and judged, and sewing or cooking skills demonstrated. The 4-H Club remains an active and positive influence on the youth of Boone County, whether they are living on a farm or in a subdivision.

This picture captures the pride felt by many Boone Countians in their work and way of life at the end of the last century. This farmer sits on his wheelbarrow, holding his Bible, after a long day of chores. During the day, he had used skills which were learned from his father and passed down through several generations. He will probably read his Bible at night by the light of a kerosene lamp.

Undoubtedly in the care of a big sister, who was busy taking the picture with her new Brownie camera, little Elizabeth McMullen watches her father, Leslie, and his helpers gather hay from the field at their Burlington farm. The McMullens are descendants of the founders of the small river community of McVille.

Harvesting the hay on an early twentieth-century Boone County farm was truly a family affair. There was a job for everyone, even the children. In this c. 1920 photograph, a child waits for the signal that the equipment inside the barn is set before she urges the horse forward to lift the hay up into the second-story loft.

Helen Stephenson poses with her horses, Daisy and Bess, while raking hay on her father's farm near Limaburg. During WW I, when many of the county's young men were called away, young women, protected from the sun by bonnets and long-sleeved dresses, did their part by helping with the farm work.

When a calf was ready to be weaned, it was necessary to teach it to drink from a bucket. Farmers sometimes used large rubber gloves with holes cut in the fingers to help a calf make the transition from its mother to feeding on its own. More solid cereal, or "calf food," was often mixed into the milk.

The inscription on the back of this photograph reads, "Jane and the cow Pap gave her." A cow given to a daughter was a practical gift, since a girl could take the cow with her when she married—or sell it. Jerseys, such as the one pictured here, were a popular dairy breed in the county. They produce milk with a high grade of butter fat.

In rural Boone county, cattle were a part everyday life. While there were farmers who owned large dairy herds, many families had only one cow for milk. Cows were named, and the bond formed between the family cows and children sometimes resulted in tears when "Bossie" had to be sold. Pictured are Alice and John Conner on their family farm on Conner Lane.

While living on a dairy farm, no matter what else happened during the day, one thing was certain. Every morning and every evening, the cows had to milked. Prior to the electric milker, all a farmer needed was a pail, a stool, and a good grip. Milking usually took place in a barn, but cows are creatures of habit and can become accustomed to being milked in any location.

Few pictures could better tell the story of daily chores on a Boone County farm. A local farmer sets off on his mower with a strong team of work horses, prepared for the challenge of a long day in the field with his wide-brimmed hat to protect him from the sun.

People who earn a living in agriculture often have a sincere regard for the farm animals that help them succeed. Boone County farmers were no different in this regard. Each cow, horse, and mule on a farm had a name, and certainly, its own distinctive personality traits. The farm bell in this c. 1940 picture has become a treasured family heirloom.

The smile on the face of young Leslie McMullen (left) reflects the joy and excitement of growing up on a farm. Young farm animals such as this Jersey calf were always fun to play with. Pictured here, from left to right, are as follows: Leslie McMullen Jr., Jeanetta Rouse, Franklin Rouse, and Lois Jones.

Once each year, in the spring, farmers cleaned out their barns and pitched the manure that had accumulated over the winter onto the fields to fertilize the coming year's crops. Horse-drawn wagons were pulled across the field while the farmer spread the manure with a pitch fork. The full use and recycling of all materials were part of a farmer's job.

Brothers Raymond (left) and Charlie Smith (right) pose with a team of mules named Pete and Dinner—two mules everyone said couldn't be broken. Dinner was a mean one, but Raymond and Charlie knew the secret to convincing him to work. Soon they had the team working daily in the Big Bone Church neighborhood of Boone County. The Smith family children included Brother Will Smith, who was later active in the county's Baptist churches.

This picture illustrates quintessential animal husbandry. Farmer Leslie McMullen made his young hogs happy by bringing them dinner. This was typical of the daily chores on a c. 1917 Boone County farm, but this photograph records a scene that is totally unfamiliar to many Boone Countians of the 1990s.

On the B.C. Kirtley farm in East Bend Bottoms, hogs sometimes made good playmates while being raised for market. Here, three-year-old Marie Kirtley enjoys a ride on the seemingly docile "Big Ted." In 1919, the 800-pound Big Ted brought $106, which was, at the time, the highest price ever paid for a Boone County hog.

With the onset of cold weather came hog killing. Farmers and their families from each community gathered to help their neighbors kill the hogs and preserve the meat needed for the following year. Pork was a staple of the Boone County diet. This picture was made at the home of Ezra Tanner, located off Hopeful Road in Florence.

Leo Flynn and his son, Dennis, residents of southern Boone County, head out for a day of work with their mules, Jack and Barney, in this c. 1945 photograph. Dennis was proud to have the opportunity to learn about farming from his father. Boone County mules worked as hard as the farmers to whom they belonged, and were rewarded with excellent care.

102

Taken from the Ohio side of the river, this early twentieth-century postcard offers an unusual view of the hillsides above Anderson Ferry. Note the nineteenth-century Boone County custom of farming the hillsides (left), and the low billboard advertisements nestled among the trees (right). Both practices would be discouraged today.

Charles Hempfling began his famous orchards along the river bottoms at Taylorsport with the purchase of Parlor Grove in 1903. He later purchased an additional 272 acres, known as Webb Hall, and became a widely known producer of apples. In this picture of the pickers harvesting the peach crop, Mr. Hempfling is the second man from the right, and his son, Liston, is third from the left.

In 1903, Charles O. Hempfling purchased the farm known as Parlor Grove, named for a popular amusement park that had flourished on that site in the last half of the nineteenth century. Mr. Hempfling was widely known as one of the largest producers of apples in this area of Kentucky, specializing in a variety known as "Big Red." Mr. Hempfling and his wife, Lillie, were the parents of three children. Their two sons, Liston and Charles, helped manage the farm. Their daughter, Anita, taught school in Boone County before moving to Baltimore. Mr. Hempfling helped form the Boone County Farm Bureau. Pictured in front of the Parlor Grove wagon are Vaughn Hempfling (center) and Liston Hempfling (right).

Barn raisings required neighborhood cooperation. The men of the community gathered to raise and secure the frame of the barn. Many were constructed using wooden pegs, which produced a securely built framework. This barn (built in 1914) no longer stands, not because of poor construction, but because of changing use for Boone County farmland.

As soon as thrashing was finished on one farm, the thrashing machine was moved to a neighboring farm to restart the process. Farmers frequently went to neighbors' farms to lend a hand, and their wives often prepared large dinners for the thrashing hands. Such large displays of food no doubt gave rise to the expression, "they've got enough food to feed a thrashin'."

In the southern part of the county near Verona, thrashing was a task often accomplished with help from your neighbors. Usually, one person owned a thrasher and went from farm to farm offering use of it for hire. Neighboring farmers helped each other harvest their crops in a timely manner.

Pictured are Charles Utz and M. M. Slayback, paused in their farm work. Like most early Boone County barns, the one seen here is constructed of logs. The earliest log barns had neither a roof nor chinking between the logs. They were designed primarily as a secure area where livestock could be penned at night to protect them from wild animals.

Feeding and caring for the family's poultry was an everyday task for both farm families and those in town. The necessity of fresh eggs and poultry meant that almost every family had a hen house and a flock of fowl. In the days when preparing a chicken dinner began at the chopping block and continued through plucking and cleaning each bird, fried chicken on Sundays was well appreciated.

"Grandma" Bertie Stephens Rector and her son, Paul, feed the chickens on their farm on Double Lick Creek, located above Rabbit Hash. Bertie and Walter Rector worked hard to provide a living for themselves and their four children on a 100-acre farm. Bertie outlived most of her family. She was buried on her 90th birthday in 1961.

After the thrashing, the straw left over was piled into stacks to be used as bedding for the animals. Before mattresses were common, people also used the straw to make bedding for themselves. Much like feather beds, straw ticks were used on beds in the nineteenth century in place of a mattress.

By the late 1800s, farmers no longer had to drop corn by hand and cover it with a hoe. Horse-drawn corn planters made the job more efficient, dropping and covering the corn as the machine moved down the row.

Boone County farmers produced as many of their daily provisions as possible. In this photo, the cane-like grass sorghum was cut, and the juice extracted, boiled, and canned. Sorghum molasses was a sweet treat that could be used like butter or jelly on biscuits, as well as in cooking and baking. Even small children could assist with the harvest process by riding the horse in a circle to power the grinder.

Early in the twentieth century, Boone County farmers began making the transition from horse-drawn vehicles to cars and tractors. Frank Rouse purchased this tractor in 1909. The caption on the picture reads, "Second tractor in Boone County. E.C. Riley owning one about six months before I owned this one."

For Boone County and the rest of the commonwealth, tobacco was an important crop in the nineteenth and twentieth centuries. Nearly every farmer raised some acreage of tobacco, ranging from a small patch to several acres. In this 1923 photograph, Judge N.E. Riddell stands in the tobacco patch of Frank Rouse on Conrad Lane, near Burlington.

In the cycle of the farmers' year, August and September brought the cutting and hanging of the tobacco crop. In this early 1920s view, farmers are shown cutting tobacco. Pictured from left to right are as follows: Hubert Rouse, J.W. Kelly, and John Clark. As with other farm jobs, neighbors in a farming community came together to offer help in cutting tobacco.

The Ohio River was often the "superhighway" for Boone County farmers to ship their goods to larger markets. In order to transport crops and receive supplies, it wasn't unusual for each farm along the river to have its own landing such as this one in East Bend Bottoms. Due to the poor condition of the roads, travel by boat was often easier and faster.

Imagine Reuben Kirtley's surprise when a WW II plane landed in his wheat field in 1944! Understandably, it was the talk of the neighborhood, and crowds came to view this unusual sight. The U.S. Army sent a crew to dismantle the plane so it could be trucked out of Boone County. The workers stayed in the large plane at night and were invited to breakfast at one of the neighboring farms.

In the early twentieth century, the Verona Grange Chapter met at the Verona High School. The Grange, originally known as Patrons of the Husbandry, was founded nationally in 1867. The first Kentucky chapter was formed in 1871. By 1875, the Grange Association had 1,540 local chapters with over 52,000 members nationwide. The Grange worked to educate and organize farmers by maintaining the law, reducing expenses, and avoiding litigation. In the 1870s, membership grew as the organization worked toward lowering transportation costs for shipping goods and developing retail co-operatives that helped farmers avoid the middleman.

Throughout 1876, letters to the editor in the *Boone County Recorder* discussed the pros and cons of the Grange. Some thought it was a secret organization designed to raise the price of goods produced by farmers. Others felt the Grange organization improved the quality of life for farmers and, interestingly, pioneered the concept of equal rights for women.

Six

BUSINESS

The post office on Main Street in Florence was located in Jim Tanner's hardware store. Notice the lanterns and other items for sale in the windows. In the days before rural delivery, people gathered each day at the post office to collect their mail and visit with neighbors. The house in which the hardware store is located still stands, but the smaller house to the right has been torn down. The building was typical of many others that began as a log cabin and later had siding added. Notice the window on the second floor: it tilts back into the house rather than sliding up. Picket fences were common and practical to keep stray animals out of yards. On the far right can be seen one of the many trees that lined both sides of Main Street well into the twentieth century.

In the 1883 Florence business references, William Henry Tanner is listed as a wagon maker and woodworker. Mr. Tanner, pictured in his Main Street shop, built and repaired wagons and carriages until his death in 1911. After the community's mode of transportation changed from horse-drawn vehicles to automobiles, the shop became the home of Martin Brothers' Garage.

The road through Florence, presently the Dixie Highway, was known as the Covington-Lexington Turnpike. Depending on the season, it could be a muddy mire or a dusty dry route. The road ranged from 16 to 20 feet in width and was covered with broken rock. Toll booths were located at various points on the turnpike. This one stood in the area of present-day Goodridge Drive in Florence.

114

In 1903, the *Boone County Recorder* reported that the Beaverlick Mercantile Company, established in 1893, may be the most prosperous commercial venture in North Kentucky. Located in the heart of Beaver, the mercantile was managed by John Taylor, with assistance from Merit Jack. In addition to housing the Beaver Post Office, the store carried a wide variety of merchandise including clothing, hardware, and seeds.

The Petersburg Dry Goods and Millinery Store was located on the northwest corner of First and Tanner Streets, beside the Christian church. In the late nineteenth century, Miss Lou Allen ran the shop, catering to the fashionable ladies of Boone County's largest community. Petersburg had a bustling economy, thanks in large part to its major industry, the Boone County Distilling Company.

Perhaps the most prevalent forms of industry in nineteenth-century Boone County were gristmills and sawmills. Gristmills, such as the Crisler-Gulley mill pictured here, were located on key points of the extensive creek systems found throughout the county and ground wheat and corn for the surrounding farming community. Gristmill sites often also provided other services such as a sawmill or a blacksmith, which allowed busy farmers to spend less time away from their agricultural responsibilities. By the mid-nineteenth century, many of Boone County's larger gristmills were steam-powered while smaller mills like the Crisler-Gulley continued to use water power. It is likely that this mill became inactive by the late nineteenth century.

In 1817, Lewis Crisler purchased a large tract of land along this portion of Gunpowder Creek. An 1834 deed refers to the mills located there. Robert Gulley bought the farm in 1917 and converted the former gristmill building to a tobacco barn. Only the stone foundation remains on the land still owned by descendants of Gulley.

Taken in the aftermath of the storm that destroyed the bridge at Limaburg in 1917, this view shows the sawmill, which was undamaged. Many mills for both lumber and grain sprang up along the numerous streams in Boone County. The mill at Limaburg was run by the Bill Waters family.

Alvin Boyers Renaker, known as A.B., grew up in Grant County but later moved to Burlington. In 1905, Renaker was appointed cashier of the Peoples Deposit Bank in Burlington and received a monthly salary of $70. Besides serving as the community banker, Renaker was the secret supporter of the "Santa Claus Fund" and had the foresight to establish a trust fund for the maintenance of the old Burlington Cemetery.

Gulley and Pettit's store, located on Jefferson Street, supplied the needs of Burlington and surrounding areas. Established at the end of WW I, the store was owned by brothers-in-law Lester Gulley and Albert Pettit. Their store carried groceries as well as hardware and farm supplies. The owners were generous and often allowed farmers to buy their goods on credit until their tobacco crops were sold.

118

This winter scene, photographed in the county seat of Burlington, features the 1889 Boone County Courthouse. It was the third courthouse built on the same site in Burlington. The first building was a c. 1800 log construction that became the center of local government. In 1817, a large brick courthouse was constructed facing what is now Jefferson Street. Finally, in 1889, a new courthouse, designed by the McDonald Brothers of Louisville, was completed for just under $20,000.

General stores stocked all types of merchandise needed by the rural community. In this c. 1925 view, Mr. Shelly Aylor stands in his store at Gunpowder, ready to serve his customers. Coca-Cola was a popular product, as the advertisement in the store shows. In the back of the store is the stove around which Mr. Aylor's regular customers gathered to warm themselves in cold weather and exchange news.

Although small in size, the community of Verona, in the southern part of Boone County, was quite prosperous in the early twentieth century. The Verona Bank, pictured here in 1930, was chartered in 1903 with a capital stock of $15,000. The small but substantial brick bank building is still a Verona landmark even though the bank business, now part of a larger institution, has moved to the edge of town.

Cashier Charles E. McNeely and assistant cashier John Clore are pictured inside the Citizens Deposit Bank of Belleview in 1930. The bank was established in 1913, and a new, state-of-the-art building was constructed in 1927. This building continues to serve the financial needs of Belleview as a branch of the Bank of Kentucky.

This general store, just west of "downtown" Constance, was in many ways the heart of the community. All kinds of goods could be purchased here, and the Constance Post Office was also housed in this large building. Interestingly, this building looks more like a fine home than a place of business. The store still stands, although in dilapidated condition, on Boone County's River Road.

Known by several names, this large brick building at the corner of First and Market Streets, was reportedly built in only three weeks c. 1892. The distinctive, cast-iron storefront on the first floor showcased a number of retail businesses. The large second floor space was used for a variety of entertainment and provided Sunday space for the Petersburg Baptist Church before the sanctuary was built c. 1913.

The last owner of the general store in Limaburg was J. Proctor "Proc" Brothers, seen here pumping gas in front of the store. The first owners were brothers Silas and Jacob Rouse. The store ownership then passed to Clark Beemon and Mr. Quigley before being purchased by Mr. Brothers. As with all general stores, a large variety of products were available for both household and farm needs. Often, if the store did not have the desired items in stock, the owner would travel to Covington to order them. Children often had to make difficult choices with the variety of penny candies offered. The store was the heart of Limaburg until it closed in the late 1950s.

In 1925, the Boone County Deposit Bank, established in 1885 as the first bank in Boone County, built a new building across from the courthouse. In order to construct the bank here, the c. 1837 county clerk's office was moved to a new site just west of the main intersection. Pictured is the lobby of the bank during grand opening festivities. The building now houses the Boone County Planning Commission.

The Rabbit Hash Ferry crossed the Ohio River between Rabbit Hash and Rising Sun, Indiana. The Rabbit Hash Post Office was once called Carlton. Mail was then delivered by steamboat, and Carlton was often confused with Carrollton, farther down river. In order to avoid the confusion, the name was changed to Rabbit Hash. In the early 1800s, the main route between Cincinnati and Vincennes went through Burlington, crossed the river from Rabbit Hash to Rising Sun, and went on to Vincennes.

In 1913, the Petersburg General Store was built on the corner of First and Tanner Streets. The general store was constructed of brick salvaged from the 1910 demolition of distillery warehouses. The second floor of this building was the Oddfellows Hall, as indicated by a plaque above the second story. It is likely that the group paid for the building of this structure.

124

View of Ohio R. from Ky. side   near Constance, Ky.

The Ohio River has always played an important role in the life of Boone County. From the beginning, it was an important transportation route used by the early settlers. Steamboats on the river facilitated the transportation of passengers and cargo. From the earliest times, the magnificent views of the river made it a popular place for outings and picnics. Ferries connected the Kentucky river communities with those on the northern banks, and many students went by boat each day to school in Ohio. Many families whose farms bordered the river had their own private wharves to ease loading crops such as tobacco or livestock for shipment to market. In the days before pollution made it unadvisable, fishing in the river provided day-long recreation.

FAMILY NAME INDEX

Ralph	40	Daniel	39	Fannie	39
Randall		Robert	39	Jessie	33
Gertrude	42	Sayre		Russell	39
Rector		Mabel	85	Una	33
Bertie Stephens	107	Dr. Frank	85	Vaughn	
Paul	107	Sebastian		Ransom	38
Reeves		John	42	Vice	
Bessie	42	Shinkle	46	Cline	67
Mrs.	90	Siekman		Keith	67
Vern	40	Frances	42	Elaine	39
Wyonna	40	Mildred	39	James	67
Regenbogen		Slayback		Lee Roy	67
Corky	40	M.	106	Virgil	67
Virginia	40	Sleet		Walker	
Reinhardt		Jim	86	Billy	39
Edward	42	Ward	86	Waller	
Renaker		Smith		Patty Vest	60
A.B.	118	Bob	41	William	60
Rice		Charlie	100	Walton	
Grace	89	James Gale	39	Alice	52
Wilford M.	89	Raymond	100	Bill	52
Rich		Snelling		Eliza Hunt	52
Ivan	87	John	65	Helen	52
Vera	87	Snow		Noel	10
Riddell		Mary	39	William C.	58
Clinton S.	89	Snyder		Walton	
N. E.	110	Edward	50	Joe	52
Nathaniel E.	90	Rhoda Tanner	50	Waters	
Riggs		Souther		Bill	64
Mrs.	90	Lucy Marie	42	Earl	64
Ring		Sprague		Lou	64
Joseph	39	George	42	Oliver	64
Rodamer		Stephens		Stella	64
Kenneth	40	Bessie Jones	54,61	Weaver	
Milton	42	Hiram	61	Albert "Sickem"	78
Roter		Lloyd	41,54,61	Allie	33
Allie	86	Rose	39	Betty Jo	61
Rouse		Wilton	93	Ella Adams	61
Artie	38	Stephenson		Joseph	61
Atilla	62	Lenora	63	Lewis	33
Douglas	33	Helen	95	Sarah	61
Dudley	62	John T.	63	Williams	
Edo	38	Sullivan		Bill	33
Flora	38	Tommy	39	Robert	33
Franklin	99	Tanner		Wilson	
Harry	38	Katherine	66	Joe	33
Harvey	38	Lully	47	Harry	33
Hattie	33	B. C.	47	Rachel	33
Hubert	110	Carrie	51	Wohrley	
Jeanetta	99	Cora	51	Kenneth	42
Luella B	62	Ervin	38	Wolff	
Lulu	38	Lonnie	38	Laura	33
Mary B.	62	William Henry	114	Woolet	
Richard	33,38	Tungate		Ruth	39
Robert	33	George	40	Yealey	
Roland	38	Tunning		A. M.	44
Sarah Nettie	38	Alice	40	Mr.	43
Sidney	38	Twinkle		Yelton	
Stella	26	Reverend	83	Alice	91
Sterling	2	Utz		Dr. M. A.	91
Susan Crigler	49	Bee	33	Zimmer	
Wendell	86	Charles	106	Mrs.	90
Will	33	Claud	33	Zimmerman	
Ryle		Dell	33	Mrs.	19

www.ingramcontent.com/pod-product-compliance
Lightning Source LLC
Chambersburg PA
CBHW080850100426
42812CB00007B/1980